# Woodworking
## 15 D.I.Y. Picture Frame Projects

All photos used in this book, including the cover photo were made available under a Attribution 2.0 Generic (CC BY 2.0) and sourced from Flickr.

Copyright 2017. All rights reserved

Table of content

Introduction ..................................................................................................................4

Chapter 1 – Simple Frames ........................................................................................5

Chapter 2 – Inclusive Frames ..................................................................................10

Chapter 3 – Multi-Frames ........................................................................................14

Chapter 4 – Unique Frames .....................................................................................19

Chapter 5 – Artistic Frames .....................................................................................24

Conclusion ...............................................................................................................27

# Introduction

Welcome to 15 D.I.Y. Picture Frame Projects, a book designed to not only show you how to make picture frames yourself but also how to use them in order to create cherished, unique, and, sometimes, just plain strange picture frames. Everything from using them as bookends to hanging jewelry out of them, we'll help make sure you can reuse old frames and maybe create some new frames to brighten up any section of the house. Let's begin.

In the first chapter we'll get straight down to the basics, going over such things as:

- How to make a Classic Frame
- How to make an Oval or Circular Frame.
- How to make a Box Frame

Then, in the remaining chapters, we'll go over numerous types of projects such as creating inclusion frames, which are frames inside of frames, and rustic frames. We'll also cover how to make a Multi Frame that shows the Love of whoever you want in four frames. Additionally, we'll talk about some design options and how to handle some of the wood if you're inexperienced with woodworking. To help ensure you can get the most *wood* features out of your wood, we include how to provide a rustic look to any frame that you want as well.

In the last few chapters, we'll cover how to:

- Make a Jewelry Hanging cases the easy way along with an optional stand for it to lean on.
- How to turn rocks into a design pattern that you might just fall in love with
- How to turn an old frame into a whiteboard.

This book has a lot of projects specifically targeting frames, both in building them and in designing more alluring frames for those who want to have unique frames or want to sell unique frames.

## Chapter 1 – Simple Frames

Simple frames refer to frames that are not complex to make and are good for beginners who have just begun to make their own items. This includes the classic picture frame, the oval or circular frames, and even some of the box frames some people prefer to use.

### *The Classic Picture Frame*

The important part about making a classic picture frame is understanding the size of the picture that will go inside of the frame as it determines the measurements of the frame. You will then need to order a piece of glass, this is usually fairly cheap, that is one inch added to the width and the height of the picture. For smaller pictures where an inch takes up a lot of the frame, you might want to look into using plastic instead so that you have a light frame and the plastic can be cut to the dimensions by hand. Another more flexible option is to go with an acrylic sheet, which you can cut to the needed dimensions and it gives you the same effect as glass with less risk. It may take some time for the glass to arrive at the shop if they don't have it inventory. This is okay as you can use this time to make the pieces of the frame.

For this next part, you will need two pieces of wood that's five times the height of the picture in length. The first piece of wood can be as thick as you want it, but the usual size is around a half inch or lower. The second piece of would should only be half the thickness of the first piece of would and should cover the one inch you added to the glass from the dimensions of the picture. You're going to take the second piece of wood by the side and glue it to one long side of the first piece of wood near one of the edges. The second piece of wood serves to keep the picture inside of the frame and prevents the glass from falling out.

Once the glue has dried, you can then begin cutting into the wood. At one end of the board and on the face of the board, cut the wood in a 45 degree angle from the edge. Place the image's corner next to the frame's new edge with the image lined up against the wood and mark the vertical opposite corner. Draw a 45 degree line from that mark upward and at that endpoint draw another line in a 45 degree angle going to the other side. Cut along both of those lines and repeat this process one more time with the same edge of the picture as you used before. Then you can do this process again, using the perpendicular edge of the picture and this will account for the height and width of the picture.

Since you can't very well put a nail in it without some bit of the nail (or screw) not have enough inside of one of the sticks, it's time to use a dowel rod. First, line up the angles so that your frame bits make a square and then glue those together. Then, use a vice to hold the frame still while you drill a hole through both angles on the frame. Push the dowel rod through these holes and then glue them in place by pulling the rod out a little bit on each side, applying glue, and then shove the glue side back in. You can hold the sticks in place by wrapping a tight rubber band around the bottoms of adjacent dowel rods. Once the glue has dried, you can then cut off the ends and sand it down.

## The Oval Frame

The oval frame is made similar to that of a classic frame but with a bit of a difference. The oval frame is not that difficult to make either. Unlike the previous one, we will be cutting the picture to fit inside of the frame since it is easier to do it like this. First you hammer in two nails that are half a foot apart from each other but level horizontally. Then you take some string or yarn and wrap it around the nails. Tie a knot around the layers of string so that it doesn't resize itself when you pull on it. A slipknot will often work with this, but any knot you prefer is okay too. Then take out the nails and hammer one in on the halfway point between the holes that the two nails left behind. Place the string around this nail and then use a pencil to draw a circular line using the string as you pull it around. You need another string that is half an inch longer than the previous string and you will do the same thing with this string. This will serve as your inlet to keep the acrylic sheet from falling out.

You need another string that is three inches longer than that string. You will again need to use this string to draw your circle. Finally, use a saw to cut inwards from the bottom of the square to the first line that you made. Cut along the first line until you can go out the same hole you went in with. Stop the saw and reposition it at the other line and then cut along this line. Repeat this process until all the lines have been cut. You should now have two circular pieces of wood, some left over wood, and an oval piece of wood that can be used as a table top later on down the road. Since the inlet is currently the same thickness as the frame, you should cut this in half at the top so that you can safely trim the thickness to half of what it is. Once you have turned this one piece into four, or two of the non-matching pieces away and you should be left with your inlet. Now it is time to glue everything together and push it tightly together, holding it or using scrap wood to keep it in place while it dries. The final step is to take some scrap wood and use it to glue some more wood together, such as at the seams. Once everything is dry, you can sand it down to lower the visibility of the edges. You should now have your oval picture frame.

### *The Six Side Frame*

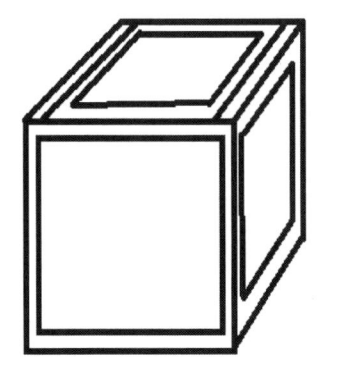

The Six Side Frame is what one would also refer to as a "box frame" since it really is a box of picture frames. Likewise, you do not have to build this frames if you don't want to but it's actually easier if you do. Follow the directions of the Classic Picture Frame in order to build six small frames that you can use and then continue on with this project.

The idea is not the frame themselves but what you choose to decorate on the frames, such as a Tron themed cubed paint or maybe going with the dots for a die. In order to make the six sided frame just have to choose six picture you will never want to remove from their frame and then glue all the frames together to make a six side frame with the pictures in the frame. That's it, it's really simple to make and this is why the design is more important than how you actually make it here.

## Chapter 2 – Inclusive Frames

Inclusive frames are frames that either hold the picture within grooves or hold another frame within grooves. These are really useful for photos that might fall apart if they were taken out of the frame they were current in or for individuals who prefer to a spark over the original frame rather than replace the frame.

### *The Square Frame*

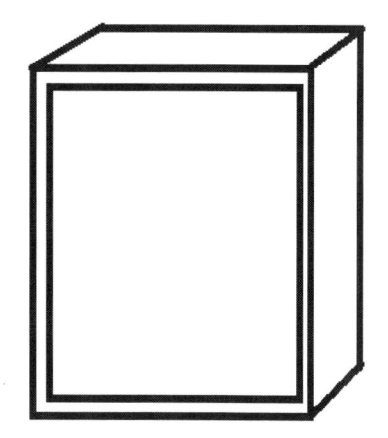

In order to make the square frame, you need to have a classic frame already built. Once you have that built, you can then begin building and inclusive structure around it. You will need four boards, two boards will as wide as the frame is tall and two more will be as wide as the frame is wide. Then you will need one last board that is the exact same size as the frame itself. Attach all the boards together via glue or nails and then get creative, because that's what this design is about. This is a great project for a family with children they might want to put a mark in their own home. As you can tell, that's an *inclusive* pun.

## The Oval Inclusive Frame

This is the same type as the previous one you just read about, but it uses a lot more wood, even if you try to cut around it. Therefore, this one should only be an inch or two thick to prevent the frame from being to heavy to lift.

All you need to do is place the frame on a thick board that is bigger than the frame and draw a line around the frame. Then you draw another line around half an inch more than this, or less if you prefer. It is okay if you do not get this perfect as it just adds to the frame. First you cut the first mark so that you have your oval and then you also cut the second mark, but don't get rid of the wood inside. Instead, you're going to pull some of it out so that the frame can go in. The part that you pull out can be cut off and used for something else. The part that you didn't pull out should be left inside and it can be secured via wood. If you want to go with the smaller piece that you pulled out, you can but this requires that you also secure the frame as you wouldn't need to if you made the fit tight enough. If you didn't, this is the better option to go with.

### The Rustic Frame

This one is really just making the frame much bigger, but in a cooler way. You will need one board that is two to three inches wide while also being one and a half times long than all the lengths of the frame. You will need another that is two times as long. You will also need to soak some steel wool in some apple cider vinegar for at least a couple of hours if not days, depending on how rustic you want it to look.

At one end of the first board and on the face of the board, cut the wood in a 45 degree angle from the edge. Place the frame's corner next to the new edge with the image lined up against the wood and mark the vertical opposite corner. Draw a 45 degree line from that mark upward and at that endpoint draw another line in a 45 degree angle going to the other side. Cut along both of those lines and repeat this process one more time with the same edge of the frame as you used before. Then you can do this process again, using the perpendicular edge of the frame and this will account for the height and width of the frame.

With the second or "last" board, it is a little bit different as we will cut via the side of the board and not the face of the board. Otherwise, we will do it the same way. Then we just use some glue to attach everything together. If you want, you can use dowel rods as we did in the Classic Frame project, but I'm going to continue on to making it look rustic. Take the steel wool that has been sitting there for a while and scrub it on the frame. The more you scrub the more it will become rustic. The vinegar oxidizes the steel wool, which causes the rust to settle in, which you pass on to the wood.

## Chapter 3 – Multi-Frames

Multi-frames refers to a picture holder that holds more than one type of picture. An example of this is the classic "Love" design, which holds a picture for each of the letters of the frame. This is for individuals who have a lot of photos to show off but want to scrunch down on the space used in between photos.

### *The Duo Frame*

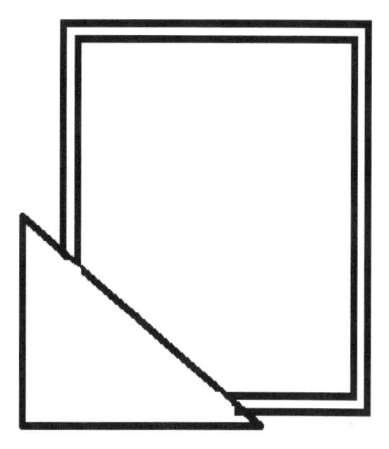

The duo frame is another simple one to make since all you need is two picture frames, but it's how you put them together that makes them different. For example, you could screw a hook into the top of each one and hanging them on the string, which could be used as the smile for a smiley face on the wall.

Another example of how a Duo Frame could be used to showcase some unique love is if you decided to use them bookends. This is not as common as it used to be, primarily because of the modern age, but bookends still make great decorations and repurposing some older books to add to the project will often show a symbolism that the relationship has been good and going on for a long time. This is great for family photos or long friendships.

All you have to do to make it is grab a one foot by three inches and one inch thick. Cut two triangular blocks out of it at a 45 degree angle using the ends of the board. Then, use a saw to cut a groove thick enough to fit the picture frame inside of it. Place the picture inside of it and it should now work as a bookend.

**The Four Way Frame**

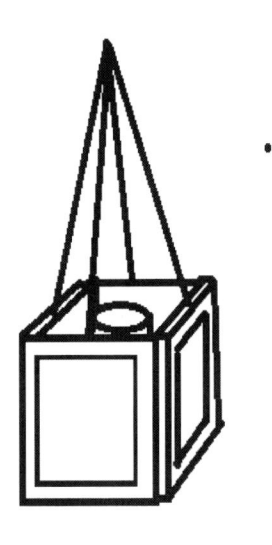

The four way frame is basically just a duo frame twice, but you see this commonly through all of the different types of frames. The most common of these is just putting four frames together to make a square, but an interest project is to make a candle out of it and all you need a four medium sized frames that are as tall as the candle you want to place them around. This makes a great addition in the house and is fairly simple to make.

The project I prefer is the one where this candle hangs from the ceiling. To do this, you can grab a square board and screw the frames into it. Then you take screw hooks and screw those into the middle of the top of each frame and then you also place a screw hook in the ceiling, positioned in a place that you prefer the candle to hang. This next step is optional, but I find that using chains to have a much greater tension strength than strings but if you want to make it some fancy design then just make sure you make sure it is strong. Either way, they all need to be the same length in order for this to work. All you have to do is tie or hook unto the hooks and then attach it to the bigger hook on the ceiling.

These work great as hanging lights and will be wonderful in times of emergency. The light is bounce and directed towards the ceiling so it has a much stronger effect and then it disperses over the room. This creates a well lit area for whoever is in the room and this is also part of the reason old-time lights like candles had reflective glass, which enhances the light depending on the glass.

***The Love Frame***

There are several ways to do the Love Frame, but we're going to go with the easiest one since we don't want to stray too far away from the frames. You will need four frames of a color you like and then four clear sheets with the letters love on them. If you don't know how to get the letters on to a clear sheet, that's okay because I'll tell you how.

You will need packing tape, preferably as wide as possible. Then you need a piece of paper that spells out the word LOVE in whatever font you want. Just make sure that these letters are evenly spaced out because you will need to cut them out. By the way, you need to put packing tape over those pieces and cut them out with some scissors or an exacto knife. Then you will need a cup or a bowl of warm to hot water. Place the letters inside of the bowl and allow them to soak up the water for a few minutes. Then take one of the letters out and begin rubbing the paper off gently. This process will be slow and if it looks like the paper is going to be dry then you need to soak them again. Eventually, you will get four pieces of packing tape with transparent letters on them. You can now put these on the outside of the frame. You can also reverse the position of the letters when you first print them out to ensure that you can put the tape on the inside of the frame.

Preferably, you want to place this in the corner of the frame as this will not block it. Additionally, you can do this will much bigger letters but then you wouldn't be able to put pictures into the frames without blocking a good portion of the picture.

## Chapter 4 – Unique Frames

This sections is dedicated for the frames that you often find on Etsy or a specialty network where individuals craft something they originally think of rather than creating something from an instruction manual. These are the odd balls that have niche uses, but they're still cool to build and sell rather well if you're in the trade.

### The Crescent Frame

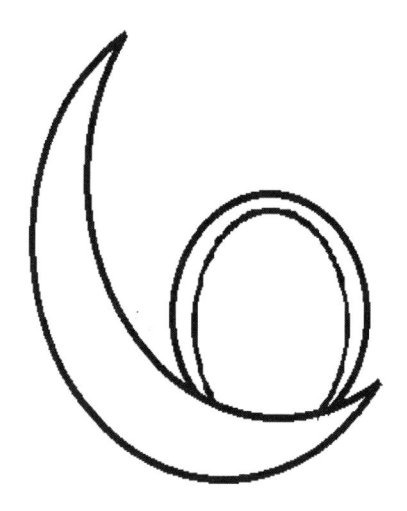

The Crescent frame is a bit deceiving when you first look at it as it looks like it is just one frame, but it is really two frames. To make this frame, you need to make an extremely thin oval frame and only half of a bigger oval frame, so let's begin.

To start, crop the picture that you want to use into a circle. Then print it out if it is not already printed. Place this image on a thin piece of wood that is either one fourth of an inch thick or one either of an inch thick. Trace the edges around the image to get the first mark that you need to begin. Then, remove the image and use a ruler to find the middle mark of the circle. Hammer in a nail at that spot and tie a string to it. Pull the string out to the mark that you just made and cut the string a few millimeters smaller than the first mark.

Finally, use a saw to cut inwards from the bottom of the square to the first line that you made. Cut along the first line until you can go out the same hole you went in with. Stop the saw and reposition it at the other line and then cut along this line. Repeat this process until all the lines have been cut. You should now have two circular pieces of wood and some left over wood. Since the inlet is currently the same thickness as the frame, you should cut this in half at the top so that you can safely trim the thickness to half of what it is. Once you have turned this one piece into four, or two of the non-matching pieces away and you should be left with your inlet. Now it is time to glue everything together and push it tightly together, holding it or using scrap wood to keep it in place while it dries. The final step is to take some scrap wood and use it to glue some more wood together, such as at the seams. Once everything is dry, you can sand it down to lower the visibility of the edges. You should now have your oval picture frame.

Now that you have this, you should still have some leftover wood from the oval frame that you just made. You can put the string in the middle of the opening that was left over and draw half a line with it. Then you need to move it towards the line by an inch and make another line that matches it. You will need to cut this out of the leftover wood. Unlike the previous one, you just need to cut a groove into this crescent wood by using a circular saw blade that is a little thicker than the oval frame that you have. Once you have done this, you can pour some glue into the groove and place the oval inside of the groove.Hold the oval so that the glue gets on it and then wait for it to dry, which shouldn't take long and you will know it is dry because it should stay still when you let it go. To make it more secure you can screw it in from the side, put a dowel rod in it, and then sand that down.

**A Whiteboard For All**

To make a whiteboard out of a frame is incredibly easy to do that almost anyone who learns how to do it is often surprised that they didn't know this before. Just put a white piece of paper in the frame. That's it, it's that simple. Well, you should also probably instead a backboard too to prevent the paper from bending but this is all that is needed to make a whiteboard. To make it bigger, you just scale it to size but this is perfect for repurposes an unused frame that's collecting dust. Now you just need a dry marker that's meant for whiteboards. If the glass is not providing enough friction, you can replace it with cardboard covered in white packing tape or clear packing tape over a white piece of paper that's on top of cardboard.

## The Jewelry Holder

Alright, so you want to make a jewelry frame. This is a frame that will let you hang jewelry inside of it, provided that it is a ring or a necklace. You often see these types of frames at the jewelry store when they have a lot of jewelry to display. Meanwhile the expensive jewelry will usually get its own show casing.

You just need a classic frame for this, a board that can fit into the frame, some black loose padding that you can put small things through, clear glue and some pretty good looking screw hooks. Place the padding inside of the frame and place some glue on the edges of the padding. Use the board to press down on the net so that the glue is squished into more places and then leave the wood. Disperse the hooks into the padding however you like and now you are done. Optionally, you can add a pole in the back (cut at an angle) to provide some support but you could just as easily lean this up against something and you would get plent of the support that you need.

## Chapter 5 – Artistic Frames

This section is reserved for a few designs that are more artistic than functional, but also still explainable inside of a book rather than a video.

### *A Showing of the Old Ways*

For this, you will need one Classic Frame, some wires, some clothespins and some rather small nails **and** screws. Hammer in the nails from the back and then wrap the wire around one of the nails, bringing it across the frame to wrap around the parallel nail. Bring the wire down to wrap the next nail and then bring it across the frame to wrap around the parallel frame. Repeat this for as many nails as you nailed in. You can, but this is entirely optional, print out the photos in black and white. Then hung up the photos on the wire lines with the clothespins. Likewise, you can add a rustic touch to it by soaking some wool steel in some vinegar or apple vinegar, your choice, for a few hours and then brushing it on to the frame and wires. This gives the feel that the frame is very old and so are the photos. You can also replace the wire with some rope to give it a little bit older look.

**A Rocky World**

You are going to need a lot of glue for this and a collection of rocks that you like as well. All you need to do for this is glue the rocks to a Classic Frame of your choice. Now, a second option around this is you can build a containing box around the outer sides and the inner sides to allow the rocks to stand inside of the container and you can keep the rocks in there by setting some glass in a groove, but this is entirely up to you and your creative mind.

### *A Hanging Garden Frame*

To begin with, this is a frame primarily only because it is shaped like a frame, which is why this project is in the artistic section. Additionally, if you have an unused frame and a plant that needs hanging then you're all the better for having these items as we will need them. Otherwise, you will need to go to the Classic Frame and build one if you don't have one already.

Then you need two blocks that are longer than the width of the frame. Line these up and drills holes in them so that they are exactly parallel to each other. Measure the distance between the holes and drill the same holes into where you would like to install these boards. Take a few dowel rods and lather them in glue. These dowel rods should be the same size as these holes or a little smaller. A different way that you can do this is fill up each of the holes with glue and place the dowel rod inside, one piece of wood at a time as each one finishes up drying. Either way, you will have the base of your hanging Garden Frame. After you do this, you can then place a screw hook in the top part of the frame and hang the plant on the hook with a pot that has chains running through handles preferably. This is more of an artistic piece since you can only hang one plant at a time, but the unique look of this type of hanging garden is certainly going to be something that draws eyes to it. There are other woodworking ways to do this, this was just the way that I chose to describe how to do it.

# Conclusion

Welcome to the end of this book and while this is the end of the project, that doesn't mean that it is the end of what you can do with picture frames. Pictures frames have a lot of uses, both old and new. It's up to you to see how far you can go.

# FREE Bonus Reminder

If you have not grabbed it yet, please go ahead and download your special bonus report *"DIY Projects. 13 Useful & Easy To Make DIY Projects To Save Money & Improve Your Home!"*

Simply Click the Button Below

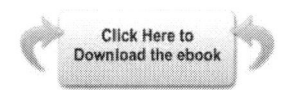

OR **Go to This Page**

http://diyhomecraft.com/free

## BONUS #2: More Free & Discounted Books or Products

**Do you want to receive more Free/Discounted Books or Products?**

We have a mailing list where we send out our new Books or Products when they go free or with a discount on Amazon. Click on the link below to sign up for Free & Discount Book & Product Promotions.

**=> Sign Up for Free & Discount Book & Product Promotions <=**

OR Go to this URL

**http://zbit.ly/1WBb1Ek**

Manufactured by Amazon.ca
Bolton, ON

Manufactured by Amazon.ca
Bolton, ON